The Officer's Family Social Guide

By Mary Preston Gross

Beau Lac Publishers
Box 248
Chuluota, Fla. 32766

BOOKS BY MARY PRESTON GROSS

MRS. LIEUTENANT
MRS. FIELD GRADE
MRS. NCO
MILITARY WEDDINGS AND THE MILITARY BALL

Library of Congress Catalog Card No. 77-72724
ISBN:
Paperback 0-911980-07-5
Hard Cover 0-91198-08-3

Beau Lac Publishers
P. O. Box 248
Chuluota, Florida
32766

THE OFFICER'S
FAMILY SOCIAL GUIDE

TABLE OF CONTENTS

TO

MIKE

AND

ELLIEWOOD

FOREWORD

This book was written for people who want simple and direct answers to questions pertaining to military customs and traditions. It details courtesies and protocol that officers and their families need to know. Parts of it have been directed to the wives since they usually assume the family's social responsibilities.

The different branches of the services have customs and traditions that have grown with them. The purpose of most of them is to help you and your family to be happy and to adjust quickly and comfortably when making friends in a new community.

Your practice of these customs will enable you to avoid misunderstandings and uncertain moments that are apt to arise when you unintentionally disregard a custom or tradition.

In addition, being knowledgeable of these customs will help you to consider the feelings of others and to be understanding and sympathetic with those who need your friendship because they are less informed and less at ease than you are.

If older couples have patience with younger couples and help them learn the ways of the military, it will be easier for the younger couples to accept and appreciate military customs. A family new to the service should remember that the senior families understand their position as they too were once new to the service.

Protocol is the practice of customs that say who does what first and where. The rules have not been dreamed up simply to stress snobbery, but have grown from orderly and systematic behavior when showing consideration for the feelings of others. They inspire one to do the natural and unselfish thing.

This book is not intended to encourage you to follow unnecessarily in the footsteps of others and lose your identity. Its aim is to help you develop your own personality and have confidence in your own behavior. Society has at last agreed that socially and within reason, one should feel free to do and act as one is so inclined.

The degree of formality within a particular branch of the service, will vary according to the post or base. If you are stationed at a base where informality is the thing, it is indeed naive to assume that it will be the same way at your next assignment. The social tempo is generally determined by the commanding officer and varies from a lax, informal manner of living at a small post to the more formal, sophisticated life at a large installation.

In recent years the gap between the social lives of the commissioned and noncommissioned officers' families has been shortened and today, on occasion, they intermingle socially. This has aided significantly in making military life more friendly now than ever before.

In this book we have not mentioned protocol or customs used in the diplomatic corps. In some respects they differ and should not be confused. When stationed in or near the District of Columbia, where the military and diplomatic corps are apt to mingle, the military usually defers to State Department customs.

If you find yourself involved with State Department protocol, there are several good books written specifically for and usually by people in the State Department. If you are the recipient of an invitation to the White House, telephone or write to one of the social secretaries and ask the necessary questions.

In many instances we have stressed the more formal manner of doing things. This does not mean that you can not or should not have back-yard barbecues, picnics and other forms of informal parties.

However, since service families are more apt to find themselves, on occasion, involved in the more formal manner of living, officers and their families are expected to know the rules and to be as poised and as much at ease at a formal reception as they would be at a pool-side party. Poise is acquired by knowing what to do when, and being normal and natural while doing it.

In addition, there are a few rules stated in this book that are occasionally broken. For instance, we say that a lady need not stand when a gentleman enters the room. However, she DOES stand for the President of the United States, a reigning king, or a high church dignitary. Inasmuch as these occasions are the exceptions, we have omitted them.

Information on weddings has been omitted. Our book, MILITARY WEDDINGS AND THE MILITARY BALL, will tell you what you need to know.

In the military there are noncommissioned officers, commissioned officers, and in some branches, warrant officers.

There are nine steps in the noncommissioned ranks, E 1 through E 9. It is advisable that all family members know these ranks and are able to identify enlisted rank insignia.

Warrant officers have four steps.

In the Army, Marine Corps, and Air Force, commissioned officers, of which there are ten grades, are categorized as *company grade* officers, (second lieutenants, first lieutenants, and captains) *field grade* officers, (majors, lieutenant colonels, and colonels) and *general officers.* Field grade and general officers are sometimes refered to as "senior grade" officers. In the Navy, *junior grade* officers are ensigns, lieutenants junior grade, lieutenants, and lieutenant commanders. Commanders, captains, and admirals (flag officers) are *senior grade* officers.

A company, or junior grade officer's family must be able to meld successfully into an already established way of life. When they arrive at a base or post, the other members of the command will extend to them all of the courtesies and privileges that are given to all military families. The chief of security or provost marshall will be as interested in their security as that of the senior family; the engineers will be as interested in the maintenance of their quarters, and the commander as interested in their well being. A wise couple will show their appreciation and reciprocate by making a real effort to cooperate and become a part of the community. They will learn and use the customs of the services as detailed in this book. They will play the game according to the rules and allow living with the military to be the wonderful experience it is meant to be.

If, for some reason, an officer should return to civilian life, the military record could be the only recommendation and reference. It will certainly be more advantageous if the record reflects a couple who were sincere in their efforts, who could meet and enjoy new people, who were able to adapt to new and different circumstances, and who displayed an attitude of cooperation and respect.

Many think that the field grade officer and spouse are the most vital link in the military life chain. They are the bridge between the young and the old, the inexperienced and the experienced, and in some instances, the insecure rank and the secure rank. Some cross the bridge and soon forget that they too, were once on the other side, while others take with them the mistakes, the tears, the successes, the joys, and pass them on to newer and younger couples. Most have learned and understand the give and take of military life and how to cope with and overlook irritations and pettinesses.

Someone once said that there is no rank among women. Let us stress here that it is true that a wife has no military rank and should not tell another woman what to do simply because her husband is senior to the other woman's husband. However, she does have position which is created by her husband's rank. Eventually, most young wives will be the "ranking lady" and will appreciate and need the support and respect given to her position.

Official precedence is binding on all members of the federal government and within these parameters, wives take precedence from their husbands. If one remembers to treat older persons with formality and respect, "respect to rank" is usually the result. One cannot deny that there is rank among all living creatures, sometimes known by other names; status, position, age, pecking order, etc. It is true that a mother out-ranks her children, and that our President's wife is our First Lady.

Do not let the knowledge derived from this book encourage you to become a "finder of faults" in others. Its purpose is not to stimulate criticism, but enable us to eliminate frustration and discord and to enjoy together the many exciting and interesting experiences offered to a military family.

Social customs are cultivated through man's effort to make his companions comfortable and happy. Rules may be learned, but graciousness is developed by living with kind thoughts and consideration for others.

Tact, a sense of humor, and responsibility for and to others will stand any family in good stead.

So, as you read this, be proud of the fact that you are making an effort to contribute to the esprit de corps that is developed when we serve with the armed forces of our wonderful United States as part of a happy, congenial and proud family.

TRADITIONS

One of the old traditions that has withstood the test of time, is that of newly-appointed officers giving a dollar bill to the first enlisted person who salutes them after they have received their commission.

If an officer, senior in rank, has said, "I wish" or "I would like," it is comparable to a direct order.

When a choice is to be made, the senior officer has the priority, not "first come, first served."

When an officer speaks of the commander as the "Old Man," this is not disrespectful. It is used because of position, not age, and usually is an expression of admiration. However, it is never used in the commander's presence.

The term "service brat" is not name calling, but a term of endearment given to children born and raised in the service.

Soldiers, sailors and airmen are not "boys" or "girls." They are men and women doing adult jobs.

It is a longstanding Army tradition that male officers do not carry umbrellas when in uniform. However, female officers are authorized to use them at any time except when in formation. In the Air Force, they may be used by both male and female officers except when in formation.

Do not speak of a FULL colonel. There is no such rank. The officer is either a lieutenant colonel or a colonel - both usually full of good will.

When writing a social letter to a Lieutenant Colonel, the envelope should be addressed to Lieutenant Colonel, but the saluation should be, Dear Colonel.

Some like to speak of doctors, lawyers, etc., as professionals. All officers are professionals. Who could be more professional than the man who has dedicated his whole life to the defense of his country?

When introducing a Navy captain, when among officers of other branches of the services, say, "Captain, United States Navy."

Aboard ship, the officer in charge of the ship is always called "Captain," regardless of his rank.

Under most circumstances, the rules that apply to male officers, also apply to female officers. An exception is when attending a graveside funeral. Male officers remove their hats and female officers do not.

The ranking officer always sits on the right side of the back seat of an automobile. When entering from the curb side of the car, the junior officer opens the door, the senior officer is seated, and the junior officer goes around the car and enters on the left side. In heavily congested traffic, the junior officer opens the door, enters first, and moves to the left side, leaving the right seat for the senior officer.

The same applies when a non-military spouse accompanies an officer. The spouse enters first and slides over to the left side, leaving the right back seat for the officer.

When walking, the position of the junior is to the left of the senior. Seniors precede juniors through entranceways.

When a commissioned officer and his family are stationed with another branch of the services, the entire family is expected to adhere to the customs of that branch.

A newly promoted officer almost always has a promotion party. Although traditionally it was given on the first payday after the promotion it can be given whenever practicable. In the Navy it is called a Wetting Down.

It is as important for a single officer to adhere to social customs as it is for a married couple. This includes answering invitations, sending "thank you" notes, and repaying social obligations. Frequently several singles pool their guest lists, share the expenses, and hold some sort of affair at the club.

Usually a general or flag officer's flag is flown on the headquarters building when he is in his office and lowered when he leaves the building.

The star plate exposed on an official car means that a general or flag officer is in the car. The plate is covered when the officer is not in the car. The same applies to the commanding officer of a unit. If you see a unit insignia on the car, you will know that the commanding officer of that unit is in the car. In like manner, it is covered when he is not in the car.

If there is a sentry or guard at the entrance of a military installation, your commissioned officer's car sticker will be recognized and you will receive a salute. Officers return the salute but a dependant driving the car without an officer in it simply smiles, nods, and quietly says "Thank you".

Usually there will be reserved parking places at the commissary, exchange, clubs, theater, and other public places for cars of flag officers, 06 officers, certain senior enlisted persons, the handicapped and those who have certain positions. Respect these places and don't use them unless your car has a sticker showing entitlement; then DO use them so as not to take a space elsewhere from someone who is not privileged to use reserved parking.

Make appointments to see at their offices the doctor, lawyer, base engineer, and other people who give personal assistance. Do not take advantage of the fact that they are your neighbors and disturb them at home. They too are entitled to privacy.

Some bases and posts have an excellent sponsor program. An officer of the same rank or age group, is asked to assist the incoming officer and family in getting settled at the new assignment. The sponsor might meet the new officer on arrival, have temporary or permanent quarters reserved, beds made up, basic foods and supplies (with a receipt which should be reimbursed immediately) and possibly dinner ready for their first night. The sponsor continues to assist the new officer and family until they are settled and can be on their own.

Most posts and bases have a volunteer organization called Community Services where a new officer's family may obtain information on the services available on post.

Commissary and Exchange privileges are traditionally considered when establishing military pay scales. It is both illegal and immoral to shop at either place for your unauthorized friends or relatives. You are however, allowed to buy bona fide gifts at the Exchange. These fringe benefits are privileges that you earn only for yourself and your dependents. If you are asked to infringe on these rights, do not hesitate to explain why you must deny their request.

Traditionally the Officers' Open Mess and Club is the center of social activities. Sometimes membership for new arrivals is automatic although it is generally considered voluntary. Small monthly membership dues entitle you to the use of all club facilities: check cashing privileges, dining rooms, club rooms for special functions, dancing and entertainment, tennis courts, swimming pools, and frequently over night guest houses. Your membership card allows you temporary use of other officers' clubs in your branch of the services as well as the other branches. As at any private civilian club, none of these facilities may be used unless you are a member.

Unit social functions are frequently announced by a flyer sent through the distribution center. It is the officer's responsibility to see that it is delivered to the spouse. The distribution center should not be used for personal use unless it is the only intra-post system such as at certain overseas assignments.

It is an accepted fact that some sort of alcoholic drink is usually offered at most military social gatherings. This is not to imply that in order to be socially accepted it is necessary to drink alcoholic beverages. It is a personal matter and is left entirely to the individual as to whether or not to drink or to serve alcohol.

If you are offered a drink and do not want it, there is no need to accept it; nor is it necessary to give an explanation as to why you have refused it.

A newly-appointed officer will do well to be aware of all organizational social affairs and attend them if at all possible. It is best not to decline an invitation from the commanding officer unless official duties prevent your attendance.

If you are fortunate enough to be sent overseas, remember that you and your family are representatives of the United States and at the same time guests of the other country. Make an effort to learn their language and customs and don't allow yourself to become lulled into living entirely within the American community. Encourage your family to benefit from the advantages of your host country. It is an opportunity that should be used and appreciated.

In like manner, if you live on a government installation in the States, make a special effort to include local civilians in your circle of friends.

Integrity and honesty, spoken and written, in business and in personal affairs, are expected of all officers and their families.

Q. What should I do if I am driving a car and hear the cannon or music of Reveille or Retreat?

A. When in sight of the flag, moving vehicles stop. On an Army post persons in a passenger car should dismount and salute. On an Air Force or Navy base occupants of a passenger car remain seated.

Q. What is the proper way for a person not in uniform to render appropriate honors to the flag?

A. Stand at attention and place your right hand over your heart.

Q. When stationed in a foreign country, should a person not in uniform salute the foreign flag?

A. No, stand at attention with your hands at your side. Also stand when the national anthem of the foreign country is being played.

Q. Should I R.s.v.p an invitation to a military review?

A. Yes, as usually seats are reserved.

Q. How should a spouse dress for a review?

A. Wear clothing that is appropriate for the time of day. Be conservative rather than overly dressed.

Q. How do you know when the review is over?

A. The review is over when the reviewing officers have broken ranks. This happens shortly after the last troops have passed the reviewing stand, or if there is a "Fly Over," when the last plane has flown over.

FLAGS, PARADES AND REVIEWS

We hear much about flags, colors, standards, etc. For example, we speak of the colors passing in review, or a flag at half staff. "Colors" are flags carried by dismounted units. "Standards" are flags carried by mounted or motorized units. "Ensigns" are flags on ships or boats.

The National flag is raised ceremoniously each morning at Reveille and lowered each evening at Retreat. In the Army and Air Force the actual time is determined by the base commander. In the Navy, the flag is raised at 0800 hours and lowered at sundown.

If you should be walking by the flagstaff when the flag is being either hoisted or lowered, stop, face the flag, and render the appropriate honors. Maintain this stance until the flag has been positioned, or, if there is music, until the music has ceased.

Reviews and Change of Command ceremonies are considered official functions and your attendance is as important as at a reception. A personal invitation to a review should be answered promptly since seats are customarily reserved and the commander will want to know if you are attending.

The times to stand are few, but it is important that you know them and rise without hesitancy and with assurance. Stand at the first note of "Ruffles and Flourishes" (played when a general or flag officer is present), "To the Colors," the National Anthem and national anthems of other countries. The following are the beginning notes of "Ruffles and Flourishes" and "To the Colors":

Ruffles and Flourishes:

To the Colors:

14

Also, stand when the colors, passing in review, are six paces before you, and remain standing until they are six paces past you. THEN BE SEATED.

When assigned overseas, learn to recognize the host country's national anthem and stand when it is played.

Children love reviews and are always welcomed and encouraged to attend, provided that you assume the responsibility of their behaving quietly and properly.

If a seat has been reserved for you, the probability is that your children were not included in the invitation, so arrangements should be made for a friend to sit with them elsewhere.

Dogs should be kept under restraint during a review or parade.

A personal invitation to a review generally is also an invitation to the reception following, if there is to be one. Do not take your children to the reception unless they were especially invited.

Save your chatting and smoking until later as this is a patriotic function and should be treated with respect.

CHANGE OF COMMAND CEREMONY

The 666 Engineer Group
requests the pleasure of your company
at the Change of Command Ceremony
at which
Colonel William Milton Whitney
will be relieved by
Colonel John Hugh Rogers
on Friday, the tenth of April
at eleven o'clock
Ketchum Field
Fort Blank

Please reply.
363 9251

An invitation to a reception may be enclosed on a smaller card.

> *Reception*
> *immediately following the ceremony*
> *Officers' Open Mess*
> *Fort Blank*

Response Card:

> *Name* _____
> _____ *accept*
> _____ *will not be able to accept*
> *the invitation of the*
> *Commanding Officer, 666 Engineer Group*
> *to attend the*
> *Change of Command Ceremony and Reception*

Change of Command Ceremonies differ among the services. The above are suggested basic formats.

The outgoing officer normally will ask the incoming replacement for a list of his personal friends whom he would like invited to the ceremony and reception.

Invited guests should arrive fifteen minutes before the ceremony. Usually, guests will be taken to a reserved seat by an escort officer. Normally, they will be seated according to their sponsor's rank. It is permissible to chat with friends prior to the ceremony, but once the ceremony starts, talking should cease.

An effective suggestion is for the spouse of the outgoing officer to sit in the middle of the first row, directly behind the spot where the officer's command will be relinquished. The spouse of the incoming officer could be seated at the right. Then, at the moment the officers change command, the two spouses could change seats, putting the incoming officer's spouse in the center of the row and the outgoing spouse at the right. If there is a very high ranking guest who is in the reviewing stand, the guest could be given the seat at the right of the outgoing spouse, and the incoming spouse, the seat at the left.

INVITATIONS AND ACKNOWLEDGMENTS

Q. How long before a party should invitations be sent?

A. Generally speaking, ten to fourteen days before the party. During a busy social season, three weeks may be better. On the other hand, many successful, informal parties have been given on the spur of the moment.

Q. What should be on an invitation?

A. An invitation should state the kind of party, by whom given, the place, date, time and where the acceptances or regrets should be sent.

Q. Should I address an invitation or letter to "Mrs. Mary Smith" or "Mrs. John Smith?"

A. "Mrs. John Smith." "Mrs. Mary Smith" is used for a divorcee.

Q. May I use the "fill-in" cards for invitations to a formal dinner?

A. Yes. These cards are used for almost any occasion, either formal or informal.

Q. May I telephone my invitations?

A. By all means do. This is a wonderful way to invite friends to small informal parties. Be direct and to the point. When you receive an invitation by telephone, be brief. Your hostess has other calls to make.

Q. When writing or answering a formal invitation on folded note paper, should I use the front sheet or the inside sheet?

A. Use the front sheet.

Q. What is meant when "Regrets only" is on an invitation?

A. The hostess is telling you that it is unnecessary to let her know if you accept, but to notify her if you must decline. This is not a good idea from the hostess' viewpoint when she needs to know the exact number of guests to expect.

Q. What is meant by R.s.v.p.?

A. This is the abbreviation for the French phrase *"répondez s'il vous plait"* which translates, please reply. It is better to use the English phrase "Please reply." so that there will be no doubt that your guests understand that you are waiting for an answer. Whichever phrase is used, you MUST respond promptly.

Q. If an invitation states R.s.v.p. but gives no telephone number, how should I respond?

A. You should write your reply.

Q. Should I R.s.v.p. when the invitation doesn't call for it?

A. Even though an invitation may not have R.s.v.p., thoughtful guests will thank the hostess and let her know whether or not they are accepting.

Q. Must a formal invitation be answered with a formal reply?

A. Yes. It should be written in the third person in black or dark blue ink on white note paper.

Q. Is it necessary to repeat the date and time when accepting a formal invitation?

A. Yes, these are important details. If an error has been made in the invitation, it will be brought to the attention of your hostess. In declining, it is necessary to repeat only the date, not the time.

Q. May I leave an answer to an invitation with whomever answers the phone?

A. Be sure to speak to the hostess, or another adult.

Q. How should I decline on oral invitation when I have no other commitment but don't want to accept it?

A. When you do not care to accept an invitation, hide your feelings and simply say "I'm sorry, but we will not be able to come. Thank you for thinking of us."

Q. Is it necessary to answer an invitation to a wedding?

A. If the invitation includes an invitation to the reception, then it should be answered, otherwise, no.

INVITATIONS AND ACKNOWLEDGMENTS

Invitations are either formal or informal.

Formal invitations are handwritten or engraved, in the third person on white paper in black ink. They are used for official receptions, teas, luncheons, reviews, formal dinners, formal dances or balls. They should be mailed two weeks in advance and answered within twenty-four hours.

Informal invitations are usually written in the first person. They may be telephoned or written on calling cards, note paper or informals. There are many novel commercial ones that are attractive, and original home-made invitations are wonderful.

They too, should be answered in the same manner in which they were entended; if they were extended by telephone, they should be answered by telephone; if extended in writing, they should be answered in writing. If a telephone number is on a written invitation, the acknowledgment may be telephoned.

We can not stress enough the importance of answering an invitation when it has been requested and it should be done without delay. To neglect this is extremely discourteous and inconsiderate to your host and hostess. It identifies you as being naive or thoughtless and is sufficient reason for your host and hostess to omit you from their next guest list. Remember, R.s.v.p. on an invitation means that you MUST reply.

Address your invitations and acknowledgments to Lieutenant and Mrs. John Bowman, or Mrs. John Bowman when only she is invited - never Mrs. Jane Bowman.

Do not issue an invitation when you are "chatting" with a friend. It may be forgotten.

To issue an invitation to one person in front of another person whom you are not inviting, is both rude and unkind.

Take the guess work out of invitations and include all the information your guests need. Tell them WHO is inviting them to WHAT for WHOM, WHERE and WHEN, including the date and time. To mention the dress is helpful and if there are doubts, as to where you live, include a small map showing how to get to the party.

Example of Formal Invitation:

To Honor Major General and Mrs. Keith Andrews
Colonel and Mrs. William Milton Whitney
request the pleasure of your company
at dinner
on Saturday, the tenth of May
at half past seven o'clock
at the Officers' Open Mess
Able Air Force Base

Please reply.
Quarters 56

Example of Formal Invitation by an Organization:

The Officers and Ladies
of
Fort Blank
request the pleasure of your company
at a
reception and dinner in honor of
Major General and Mrs. Keith Andrews
on Saturday, the tenth of May
at half past seven o'clock
at the Officers' Open Mess
Fort Blank, Virginia

Please reply.
363-9251

Example of Fill-In Formal Invitations:

Colonel and Mrs William Whitney

request the pleasure of the company of

Major and Mrs Edwards

at dinner

on Saturday, May 10th

at 8 o'clock

Qtrs 21
Quantico, Va.

Colonel (Ret.) and Mrs. John Rex Smith
request the pleasure of the company of

Colonel and Mrs Whitney

at dinner

on Saturday, May 10th

at 8 o'clock

Telephone: 725-7574

245 Laurel Court
Maryland City, Ohio

Example of Formal Acceptance:

Colonel and Mrs William Whitney
accept with pleasure
the kind invitation of
colonel and Mrs Smith
for dinner
on Saturday the tenth of May
at eight.

Example of Formally Declining:

Major and Mrs. Craig Edwards
regret that they are unable to accept
the kind invitation of
Colonel and Mrs William Whitney
for Saturday the tenth of May

Example of Informal Invitations:

On a Calling Card:

dinner
Saturday, May 10th, 8 P.M

Colonel and Mrs. William Milton Whitney

R.s.v.p   Qtrs. 56

On Folded Note Paper:

Dear Mrs Bowman,
    Will you and Lieutenant
Bowman join us for
dinner on Saturday
May 10th at 8 P.M?
        Sincerely,
    Mary Whitney

Informal Replies:

On Note Paper:

Dear Mrs. Whitney:
    John and I would enjoy having dinner with you and Colonel Whitney on Saturday, May 10th at 8.
    Thank you for inviting us.
        Sincerely
            Jane Bowman

On Calling Cards or Informals:

We accept with pleasure
    for Saturday at 8 P.M.
        May 10th.

Lieutenant and Mrs. John Bowman

SOCIAL FUNCTIONS

Q. Which invitations are considered official and must be accepted?

A. Organizational parties and receptions, when officers' uniforms are prescribed, invitations from an officer's commanding officer, or senior officers in his line of command.

Q. When we receive an invitation to an organizational party at the club, who pays for it?

A. Expenses are generally prorated.

Q. At an official luncheon or dinner at the club, should we wait until the hostess has been seated before we sit down?

A. Yes. Wait until both the hostess and the guest of honor have been seated before you sit down. Remain seated until the honored guest, host and hostess make the gesture to depart.

Q. At a prorated dinner party at the club, if the meal isn't very good, is there anything I can do about it?

A. Only an inexperienced diner would expect a perfect meal for a large crowd at any public place. The purpose of the affair is to be with friends.

Q. Am I "boot licking" if I speak with the senior guest?

A. No. Courtesy is never influenced by rank, and you will be displaying good manners to speak to all senior persons, as well as to your junior friends. But in like manner, neither should you monopolize the senior guest.

Q. May we decline the New Year's Day reception?

A. No. You may decline only if you are out of town or sick in bed.
   An officer should attend without the spouse if the spouse is ill and can not go.

Q. While we are stationed in another country, should we entertain in the American manner or try to imitate the country's custom?

A. Entertain in the American manner. Your guest of the host country will be interested in knowing American ways.

Q. Are there any people in particular whom we should entertain?

A. Yes, your friends and those who have entertained you.

Q. What are the differences between a "cocktail party", a "cocktail buffet", and a "buffet"?

A. The main differences are the times of the parties and the types of food served. A cocktail party may start as early as 5 P.M., a cocktail buffet at 6:30, and a buffet even later. Simple hors d'oeuvres or appetizers are served at a cocktail party. An invitation to a cocktail buffet promises the guests that they will not go home hungry. A buffet is a real dinner and denotes the manner in which it will be served.

Q. If an invitation to a cocktail party does not state departure time, when should we leave?

A. You should leave within two hours. From 5 to 7 or 6 to 8 are usually considered the cocktail hours.

Q. If we have declined an invitation and later find we can go, may we?

A. No, not unless your hostess has invited you for the second time.

Q. If there are no ash trays about, does this mean that I shouldn't smoke?

A. Exactly. Don't smoke unless your hostess has provided ash trays. This could be her way of tactfully asking her guests not to smoke.

Q. When introducing a lieutenant colonel, should I shorten it and call him colonel?

A. No. Speak OF him as lieutenant colonel, but speak TO him as colonel. "This is my neighbor, Lieutenant Colonel Decker." The reply should be, "How do you do, Colonel Decker."

Q. How should a Chaplain be addressed?

A. Chaplains are addressed as Chaplain. Omit the rank.

Q. Should a dinner obligation always be repaid with a dinner?

A. Normally, a dinner obligation is repaid with a dinner, a cocktail party with a cocktail party, etc. However, common sense and economic planning must be considered. To extend yourself beyond your financial capability is not in good taste and is poor judgment. To repay an elaborate dinner with a hamburger cookout, minus apologies, is quite appropriate.

SOCIAL FUNCTIONS

When you receive an invitation to a social function it should be acknowledged within twenty-four hours, without reservations, and in a definite affirmative or negative manner. Don't be guilty of asking, "Who has been invited?" or "What will be served?" Refer to the chapter on INVITATIONS AND ACKNOWLEDGMENTS for the proper form.

Guests should be punctual. This is particularly important at receptions, military formations, luncheons and card parties. However, an invitation to an "open house," cocktail party or tea, which for example states "5 to 7," permits one to arrive and depart any time between 5 and 7. Conversely, don't arrive before the invited time. The last few minutes before a party are needed by your host and hostess.

House guests or personal friends should not be brought without an invitation from the hostess. If you have a house guest, you should decline the invitation explaining why. This leaves the hostess free to extend the invitation to your guest if it is compatible with her party plans; otherwise, she will accept your regrets.

Two car lengths should be left vacant at the entrance where a party is being held. One is for the senior officer and the other for the arrival and departure of other guests.

Immediately upon arrival, pay your respects to your host and hostess, guest of honor, senior officers and their spouses, then your other friends. It is your responsibility to approach them, not theirs to seek you. This means that lieutenants and ensigns will be especially busy. Reverse this procedure when leaving, and say good-by lastly to the host and hostess. At large receptions and gatherings when it will be impossible to speak to all, special effort should be made to speak to the senior officers in your unit.

To be a charming guest is almost as important as being a gracious host or hostess. Sometimes shy people are accused of being cold and unfriendly. If this is your problem, make an extra effort to mingle with others. You need not know a person to speak. The fact that you both are guests is sufficient reason for you to introduce yourself to whomever you do not know.

When being introduced, take time to listen, and, if need be, ask that the name be repeated. Calling a new acquaintance by name not only helps you to remember it but it is also flattering to your new friend.

Always introduce a man to a lady, a younger person to an older person and one person to a group. Say first the name of the person to whom deference is being shown, "Mrs. Whitney may I present Major Edwards?" The correct reply is, "How do you do, Major Edwards."

To make introductions smoother and more pleasant a few words of information about the people being introduced are helpful.

Gentlemen and officers always stand during introductions. A female spouse may do as she prefers. It is certainly more cordial for a hostess to stand when greeting a guest. A woman may offer her hand or not. In most countries, other than the United States, it is customary. If she extends her hand, it should always be accepted.

A firm hand shake and direct eye contact are signs of self-confidence.

Treat older people with formality and respect. Do not call an older person by the first name until you have been invited to do so. Despite the fact that today, first names are used more casually, most older people prefer new acquaintances and younger people to call them by their last names. Allow the older person to make the decision.

Never use the third person when speaking to an officer. Do not say, "Does the Colonel care for a cigarette?" Say, instead, "Colonel Whitney, would you like a cigarette?"

A wife should not speak of her husband as, "the Major," or "the Colonel." There are many majors and colonels, but only one of special importance to each of us. Call him "Bob" or "Jim" when talking to other officers and their spouses even though they may be younger. Your use of the first name is not an invitation for them to use it. More formally, you may say, "my husband." To employees, clerks in stores, etc., say Lieutenant Bowman — never "the Lietenant."

Socially a husband refers to his wife by her first name or as "my wife," not as "Mrs. Alt" or "the wife."

Conversation is most important and you should talk to as many people as possible. A good listener is well liked, but one needs to be able to start a conversation. Ask your companion a question, one that demands a graphic answer and avoid those questions that require only a yes or no reply. We in the military are fortunate as there are many varied subjects that serve as common ground among strangers. Ask about a previous assignment, children or quarters. Frequently when mentioning another post or base, mutual friends can be found.

When asked a question by a stranger, give more than a one word answer. Help create a conversation.

"Hello. I'm Jane Bowman. Are you new on base?"

"Hi. I'm Jim Alt and this is my wife Ann. Yes. We've just come from Colorado. This is a great place. Have you been here long?"

Don't criticize the new base or post at which you have just arrived. For some time it has been the home of the other guests, and they are proud of their community; they may resent unfavorable outside comments.

Avoid gossip and unkind remarks about both people and places. Written words can be erased, but spoken words can't be replaced.

If a sentence must be started with, "Do you mind if I ask you a personal question?", then don't ask it. You have already told yourself that it may be embarrassing.

Learn to accept a compliment. "Thank you," without an elaborate follow up, is sufficient.

The two phrases, thank you and excuse me, can mean much. Use them frequently.

When speaking, speak slowly and enunciate well. Don't slur your words. This is accomplished by moving the lips and forming the tones with the mouth. Your purpose in speaking is to be understood.

Don't shout, even if the conversation gets loud. Keep your voice down and try hard to be heard only by those to whom you are speaking - not by everyone in the room. A well modulated voice is the key to many a front door.

The time to leave a dinner party, unless after-dinner entertainment has been planned, is usually about an hour after the meal has ended. However, in some commands it is customary to wait until after the senior guest has left. Check with the adjutant or aide as to the local custom.

On the following day, it is a nice gesture to telephone your hostess and thank her for including you. If the party was large, it is better to put your thanks in writing.

The thoughtful couple will keep a record of courtesies extended to them and make some kind of repayment. This record is invaluable when making up the guest list for your next party.

An invitation from the commanding officer, even though you must accept, creates an obligation for you and must be repaid. Do not mistakenly think that the commanding officer has "funds" with which to enterain. This is not usually true, and your social responsibility to the community is on a par with the commander's

Learn to be a gracious receiver. Many people know the art of giving but awkwardly accept favors bestowed on them publicly. Avoid the unimaginative comments "for little old me?" or "I've never been so surprised in my life." Frequently when officers are transferred, they are given a plaque or simple keepsake. Do not expect this to happen, but plan ahead and mentally select a few sentences of thanks that can be said IF it does happen.

If an organized group has given a party in your honor, remember to thank publicly, and by name if possible, those who have done the work and planning.

Sometimes noncommissioned officers and/or wives might entertain in your honor. This very important invitation should be accepted as it affords an excellent opportunity to know better the noncommissioned families and to enhance esprit de corps.

A guest's contribution to a social function is, in most instances, as important as the efforts of the hostess. A well planned party can be ruined by dull, uncooperative, or uncongenial guests. Conversely, an impromptu, spur-of-the-moment affair can be a gigantic success if the guests are compatible and lend themselves to the occasion.

If the hostess is without help and you know her well, offer to assist her; but if she declines your offer, respect her wishes. Many times too much help creates confusion and ruins an otherwise well organized party. If she accepts your offer, be gracious and inconspicuous. Don't look or act officious or important.

When a wife visits a military installation with her V.I.P. husband, the commander's wife usually assumes the responsibility of being hostess. Luncheons, coffees, sight-seeing or shopping tours may be planned.

Prepare for your out-of-town guest a short list with identifying remarks of some of your local friends whom she will meet.

FORMAL AND OFFICIAL LUNCHEONS
AND DINNERS

Q. May I type the names on place cards?

A. Handwritten ones are in better taste.

Q. Should first names be written on them?

A. Only if there are two guests with the same last name - Colonel Whitney, Captain James Jones, Captain Tim Jones are examples.

Q. How do the guests know who their dinner partners will be?

A. Sometimes the hostess will give the gentlemen cards informing them who their partners are. At other times there will be a seating chart. It is in better taste if the women stay away from the seating chart and allow the men to locate their places. The gentleman will let himself be known to his partner. Normally he will sit at the left of his partner.

Q. If I am hostessing an official function and notice after I am seated at the head table that something needs to be done, may I slip out and attend to it?

A. No one should leave the head table after being seated. Ask a waiter to attend to the detail.

Q. Should bread and butter plates be used at a formal dinner?

A. No, although they may be used at a formal luncheon.

Q. What is the rule for using table mats versus a tablecloth?

A. Normally place mats are used for luncheons or informal dinners, table cloths for formal dinners and teas.

Q. When should I use a skirt on a table?

A. A skirt may be used to hide unattractive table legs or to dress up a buffet table. It is a "must" on the front side of an elevated head table; then it is called a "modesty skirt."

Q. Is it proper to use candles at a luncheon?

A. Candles should be used when light is needed. Omit them at morning coffees and luncheons, and save them for late afternoon or evening entertaining. They should be lighted when used.

SUGGESTED SEATING ARRANGEMENTS

In military circles the table-seating arrangements at formal dinners and luncheons are usually made according to rank. The ranking man is seated at the right of the hostess and the second ranking man at her left. An exception to this might be when there is a guest of honor, in which case the honored guest would be seated at the right of the hostess and the ranking man at her left. However, this should not be done without asking the senior man to waive his right in favor of the guest of honor. If for some reason he is not agreeable to this, the solution might be to make the ranking man the cohost.

In the case of ladies only, their places are determined by their husbands' ranks. At a woman's club luncheon, their places are determined by the offices held. See chapter entitled OFFICERS' WIVES' CLUBS.

An easy way to commence is by compiling a list of the guests, arranged according to rank or position. The commanding officer and spouse are considered the host and hostess at unit parties, even though it may be a prorated affair.

Example — G = Gentleman L = Lady

Officers only:	*Officers and their Wives:*
1. Maj. Gen. Andrews	#1G Maj. Gen. Andrews
	#1L Mrs. Andrews
2. Col. Whitney	#2G Col. Whitney
	#2L Mrs. Whitney
3. Lt. Col. Decker	#3G Lt. Col. Decker
	#3L Mrs. Decker
4. Maj. Edwards	#4G Maj. Edwards
	#4L Mrs. Edwards
5. Capt. Mills	#5G Capt. Mills
	#5L Mrs. Mills
6. Lt. Bowman	#6G Lt. Bowman
	#6L Mrs. Bowman
7. Lt. Howard	#7G Lt. Howard
	#7L Mrs. Howard
8. Lt. Alt	#8G Lt. Alt
	#8L Mrs. Alt

In order to alternate the seating of men and women, certain numbers of people will naturally work out evenly while others need special planning.

Host and hostess opposite each other, at end of table:

When the number of people is NOT a multiple of four (6, 10, 14, 18, or 22) the host and hostess can sit at opposite ends of the table and the men and women guests will automatically alternate. The lady guest of honor sits at the right of the host and the second lady at his left. The same applies at the hostess' end of the table: the male guest of honor at her right; the second officer at her left. This pattern in continued, alternating men and women, descending in rank toward the center of the table.

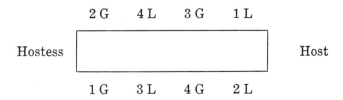

Host at one end of table, guest of honor at other:

When the number of people IS a multiple of four (8, 12, 16, 20, or 24) the guest of honor may be placed at the end of the table opposite the host. The #1 lady is seated at the right of the host and the #2 lady at his left. The #3 lady is seated at the right of the senior officer (or guest of honor) and the hostess at his left. This allows the hostess to be served last and prevents two ladies or two gentlemen from sitting next to each other.

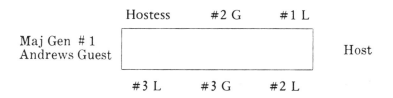

This same arrangement may be accomplished by seating the host and guest of honor across from each other in the center of the table, using the same system as above, working toward both ends of the table.

A head table is advisable when planning a large unit party or an official luncheon or dinner. It should consist of the guest of honor, host, other dignitaries and their wives. This should not exceed 10 percent of the total number of invited guests. The other guests may be seated at finger tables. At a nonmixed group, the host takes the #1 position and the senior guest the #2 seat, etc. — their seniority being determined by their rank or position.

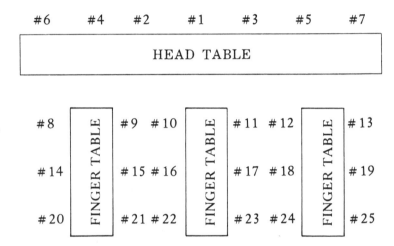

In mixed groups, the spouses of the officers are recognized according to the rank of their sponsors. If the host and hostess sit in positions #1 and #2, the male guest of honor would sit at the right of the hostess and the spouse would sit at the left of the host.

The host and guest of honor may also occupy the two center seats, with the hostess next to the guest of honor and the spouse of the guest of honor next to the host, etc., working outward toward both ends of the table.

Frequently round tables are used at both luncheons and dinners with no head table. The senior officers are scattered, one to a table, and the guest of honor usually sits at the table with the most senior officer. This mixes the ranks and makes the affair less staid.

Seldom can these arrangements be followed implicitly, but they can usually be adjusted to ensure a congenial party. Husbands and wives, if possible, should not be seated together and language barriers should be considered. Important civilian and diplomatic representatives should be melded into their proper places according to their seniority.

Try to avoid having a wife seated at the end of a head table when using only one side of a straight table. This can be done by including a bachelor as toast master or the chaplain who is to give the invocation.

Always use a modesty skirt on the front side of a head table.

If flags and colors are to be used behind the head table, see the flag arrangement in the chapter entitled RECEPTIONS AND RECEIVING LINES.

At a unit affair, when the commander and his wife are considered the official host and hostess, entertaining a high official or dignitary, the hostess and the honored male guest will enter the dining room first. The host and the dignitary's wife second. At a private party, the host and honored female guest enter first and the hostess and honored male guest, last.

DINING-IN/DINING-OUT

There is only one difference between a Dining-in and a Dining-out. A Dining-in is for officers only; a Dining-out includes spouses, dates, and guests. The main purpose of either is to boost moral and camaraderie. A Dining-out is an excellent means of welcoming new arrivals and biding farewell to those who are about to leave the command. It is held whenever the commanding officer sees the need and, as with other decisions he must make, you are expected to support him and attend.

The dress is usually mess jacket or dress uniform for officers and long dinner dresses or evening clothes for female spouses. Male civilian guests should wear suits, preferably "black tie".

The cost of the affair is usually prorated; all except those at the head table paying their share.

This well organized event varies between the services and according to the desires of the commanders, but a basic format is common to all. There is a head table, a flag line, the menu is formal and consists of beef (roast or steak) and there is a "Mr/Madam Vice".

Mr/Madam Vice is a junior officer who is selected for his wit and ability to speak. He starts the cocktail period by opening the lounge, calls the members and guests into the dining room when dinner is ready to be served, delivers the toasts, and keeps the party moving. He is seated at a table by himself and must stay until the end and leave last.

The evening is usually divided into two parts, the first being considered the formal part and the second, the informal. During the first part individual or unit achievements are recognized, new members welcomed and departing ones bid farewell. Toasts are made to people and occasions. During the second part the president (commanding officer) will turn the program over to a master of ceremonies.

Members are always punctual and arrive at the lounge within ten minutes of the time as shown on the invitation. There will be an open bar, light snacks, and an opportunity to greet the other guests. After 30 minutes or so, Mr/Madam Vice will sound the dinner bell. At this time cigarettes should be extinguished, drinks left in the lounge, and the guests move into the dining room and stand behind their chairs. The president, guest of honor, and those assigned to the head table enter last. If apappropriate, ruffles and flurishes are sounded as they march to their seats. Normally there will be a program at each place showing the agenda of the evening, toasts, menu, and other pertinent informaiton. There should be no smoking until the president indicates that the smoking lamp has been lit. This is usually during or after the serving of the dessert.

After the head table has arrived and while everyone is still standing behind their chairs, the president raps the gavel three times and calls the mess to order. If on the agenda, the Color Guard marches into the room, posts the colors and the National Anthem is played. After the departure of the Color Guard, the president asks the chaplain to deliver the invocation. The president then proposes a toast to the President of The United States. After that toast, Mr./Madam Vice usually proposes other toasts to the Secretary of the particular branch, to the Chief of Staff, etc. Then, the president seats the mess, makes his welcoming remarks, introduces by rank those at the head table with the guest speaker last. Frequently he polls the audience for introductions of other guests.

Mr./Madam Vice stands and says, "Mr. President, I propose a toast to our guests." Members stand to drink the toast but the guests remain seated and do not drink the toast. There will probably be other toasts. Gentlemen and officers stand to toast but female guests remain seated to drink the toast unless it is considered a standing ovation or they have been invited to stand. If still in doubt, the ladies should take their cues from the president's wife. If you are the person to whom the toast is being made, remain seated and do not drink the toast.

Dinner is served and there are several courses. Do not start to eat until the president has begun and allow him to start each course. When the main course has been completed, desert, coffee, and cigars are brought in and the smoking lamp is lit.

Individual and unit achievements are recognized and awards are presented. The president then introduces the speaker, if there is one, and at the conclusion of the speach Mr./Madam Vice proposes a toast to the speaker. (Gentlemen and officers rise, ladies remain seated unless invited to stand.)

There is a distinct break between the first and second parts of the affair, the formal and the informal parts. After the speech and the toasts that follow and after the president has made his closing remarks, he will adjourn the mess to the lounge. Members and guests should stand behind their chairs until those at the head table have left the room, then they too proceed to the lounge.

When the tables in the dining room have been cleared, "Mr./Madam Vice" again rings the bell whereupon the members and guests return to the dining room and again stand behind their chairs until those at the head table have returned and the president has invited all to be seated. He indicates that the smoking lamp has been lit and turns the program over to the master of ceremony for the entertainment which is to follow.

The evening comes to an end when the president has announced the conclusion of the Dining-in/out or the colors have been cased. Members should remain until the guest of honor has departed or the president has excused them. Mr./Madam Vice is the last officer to leave.

Inasmuch as there is no manditory version of the Dining-in/out the arrangements officer is not only free to but is encouraged to alter the ceremony to suit the desires of the commander. However there are a few customs that are almost always followed.

Mr./Madam Vice is the first officer to arrive and opens the lounge, rings the bell at the proper times, prepares appropriate toasts and closes the mess by leaving last.

Members and guests stand behind their chairs until asked to be seated by the president, refrain from smoking until the smoking lamp is lit, do not leave the table or return without permission, and do not start to eat a course until the president has begun.

AT THE TABLE

Q. Which utensil should I use when there are several forks and spoons at a place setting?

A. As a general rule, forks are placed at the left of the plate and knives and spoons at the right. They should be placed in the order in which they will be used, starting at the outside working towards the plate. Assuming that the table has been set properly, if you use first the utensil on the outside and work towards the plate, you will be correct.

Q. How do I know when to use a fork or when to use a spoon?

A. Never use a spoon when a fork will serve the purpose.

Q. Who starts eating first at a large organizational dinner held at the club?

A. The hostess. She, the host and guest of honor normally will be seated and served first. The hostess may start eating when those sitting near her have been served. The hostess, in this case, would be the wife of the senior man of the group sponsoring the affair. This is not to be confused with a private dinner party where the hostess is served last. Then, if it is a large party (over six guests) the hostess would suggest that her guests start eating as soon as they are served.

Q. I don't drink wine. Is it proper for me to turn my glass upside down?

A. No, it is not. Neither is it proper to cover the glass with your hand. Just say "No, thank you" to the person who is pouring. If you are ignored, don't feel obligated to drink.

Q. May I smoke at the table?

A. At the club or a public dining room one may smoke at any time. If you are a guest in someone's home, don't smoke during the meal unless the hostess has provided ash trays and then only between courses or after others have finished eating.

AT THE TABLE

We all consider our own table manners as acceptable but can easily find fault in those of others. Although this chapter may seem elementary, we will mention some of the many rules by which people are judged. Ignoring simple details at the table can be annoying and irritating to your dinner companions and create embarrassment for you.

When attending a group or organizational dinner party, do not turn down chairs or put handbags on the table to reserve places. If reserved seating is the order of the day, there will be place cards. If you are dining at someone's home, wait until the hostess tells you where to sit.

When sitting at a table with a reasonably small number of people, men remain standing until all women have been seated. When sitting at a table that seats many people, men remain standing until the women in their vicinity are seated.

Napkins are unfolded and placed on your lap. A small napkin should be fully unfolded and a large napkin left folded in half.

Don't lean over your plate but sit up reasonably straight and bring the food to your mouth, not your mouth to the food. Keep elbows and arms off the table while you are eating. However, it is permissable to rest one elbow on the table between courses or after you have eaten. Keep it close to the edge of the table and in towards your place.

Give the person sitting opposite you a break and chew with your mouth closed and don't talk with food in your mouth. If someone asks you a question while you are chewing, they will wait until you have swallowed. There should be no embarrassment and they will appreciate your thoughfulness. Probably the real answer to this predicament is never put so much food into your mouth that it can not be managed quickly.

Watch your conversation. Avoid discussing medical, dental or unpleasant subjects. Keep your talk light and uncontroversial.

Sophisticated diners never discuss the meal they are eating. Save that conversation for later.

At a dinner party, it is courteous to talk to the person at your right and your left and even across a sufficiently narrow table. No one should be monopolized or isolated.

Knives are used for cutting and spreading.

Use the butter knife to serve yourself and place the butter on your plate, not on your food. Spread the butter with your own knife, not the butter knife.

Bread or rolls should be broken in half and each bite buttered just before it is eaten. Don't use bread as a pusher and forget about bread and gravy at a dinner party.

Use the sugar spoon to serve sugar and stir with your own teaspoon. Never put your wet spoon into the sugar bowl. Don't put any utensil that has been on your plate into food that will be shared by others.

Spoons should be placed on a saucer and not left in cups, glasses, bowls, or on the table cloth. An exception: when using a large soup bowl, then leave the soup spoon in the bowl.

When eating soup, or anything from a spoon, sip from the side of the spoon, not the pointed end.

If a thin soup is served in a bouillon cup that has handles, or a small oriental-type cup, it may be sipped either from the spoon or directly from the cup using both hands.

Don't blow on food to cool it.

If salad is served as a separate course, use the salad fork. If it is served with the main course, use the same fork for both the salad and the entree. Wouldn't it seem rather silly to eat potatoes with one fork and change to another to eat tomatoes? If your salad is unmanageable with only a fork, it is permissable to cut it with a knife.

If you have used the wrong piece of silver or dropped a piece on the floor (don't pick it up) and need another, ask the waiter or your hostess to replace it.

When you have finished a course, or at the end of the meal, place your used silver across your plate. The knife and fork should be placed side by side with the tines of the fork up and the cutting edge of the knife blade faced towards you. This lets the waiter know that you are through eating.

Large, stemmed glasses are held by the bowl. Small, stemmed glasses are held by the stem. Stemmed glasses with chilled wine are held by the stem so as not to warm the wine. Brandy snifters are held in the palms in order to warm the brandy.

Cups should be held by their handles between the thumb and forefinger. When using a mug or heavy cup, it will be necessary to put your forefinger through the handle. Never wrap your hands around the cup and don't crook your little finger.

It's not proper to stir or mix foods on your plate. When eating potatoes with gravy, instead of vigorously stirring, gently twist the potato into the gravy, bite by bite.

Dunking is unattractive to watch. If you must dunk, do it at home.

Reach only for the things that you can get as easily as someone else. Ask that the others be passed to you.

If something needs to be removed from your mouth, such as a pit or bone, remove it inconspicuously with your thumb and forefinger and place it on your bread and butter plate or on your dinner plate. Never hide behind a napkin. That only attracts more attention.

One of the best ways to help improve one's table manners is to eat slowly.

Don't burp or make other unpleasant noises. Boisterous noise and loud laughter can be distrubing and embarrassing.

When you are a guest in someone's home, try to taste a little of everything that is served to you. If you have a food allergy, say nothing and leave the offender on your plate.

Don't trade food with your neighbor or scrape your plate.

Don't push your plates back or stack them. Leave them where they are, and allow the waiter to remove them.

Dessert plates may be served with a finger bowl, doily, fork, and spoon. Remove the utensils and place the fork on the table at the left and the spoon at the right. Then remove the finger bowl and doily and put them on the table above the fork. Your plate is then ready for dessert. If a finger bowl is served after dessert, don't move it but use it where it was placed. After you have finished eating, lightly dip your finger tips into the finger bowl and dry them on your napkin.

If you are in a restaurant and a friend stops by your table to chat, the men at the table stand up while the ladies remain seated.

There always seems to be the question of whether or not to stand when a toast is given. If the person offering the toast strands, then gentlemen and officers stand to drink the toast. Ladies normally remain seated and drink the toast. If the toast is considered as a standing ovation then the ladies too should stand. Everyone stands to toast the bride and groom. If there is still doubt, take your cue from your hostess and do as she does. The person to whom the toast is being made, male or female, never stands. To do otherwise would indeed be very immodest and comparable to congratulating oneself. The honored person remains seated and smiles but does not drink the toast.

If you do not drink show your respect to the honored by following the established procedure and raise your glass when the others drink.

The hostess will rise to indicate the end of the meal.

If you are using a cloth napkin at a restaurant, or if you are a guest in a home for one meal only, when you have finished eating, place the napkin beside your plate, unfolded. When you are a family member or a house guest, leave it folded. A folded napkin signifies that you will return for the next meal. Paper napkins neither should be refolded nor wadded up, but left unfolded beside your plate, not in it.

Tooth picks never should be placed on or used at the table. If they are needed, they should be used out of sight of others.

Forget your canine friend at home and don't ask for a "doggy bag" when attending a dinner party.

If the after-dinner speaker starts speaking before you have finished your dessert, you may continue eating, but make a special effort to be quiet. It isn't the eating that disturbs the speaker, but the noise. Never talk or strum your fingers while a speech is being delivered.

If you have paid your share for an organizational party, and the meal wasn't up to your expectations, don't criticize. It is a difficult task to feed a large crowd and impossible to please all.

Whenever possible, food should be eaten with a fork. However, it would be awkward and impractical not to use your fingers for certain foods.

Pickles, radishes, olives, celery, parsley, watercress and other garnishes are considered finger foods.

Crisp bacon may be eaten with the fingers but greasy soft bacon should be cut and eaten with a fork.

Large shrimps in a shrimp cocktail are impossible to cut hanging on the side of a bowl. Pick them up by the tail and bite them in half.

At a formal dinner, fried chicken should be eaten with a knife and fork. At an informal affair you may use your fingers but care should be taken to eat it tastefully and not with cannibalistic gusto.

Some eat asparagus with their fingers but since it is messy and drippy, it is better to cut off the tender ends and eat them with a fork.

Corn on the cob never should be served at a formal dinner. At informal affairs when it is served, butter and season only a few rows at a time. If you butter the whole ear, you may end up in a greasy mess.

When eating an artichoke, pull off a leaf and dip the thick fleshy

43

end into the sauce. Then place about one third of the leaf, sauce end, into your mouth. Close your teeth lightly and scrape the tasty meat from the leaf by drawing it between your teeth.

After all of the leaves have been removed, there will be a fuzzy choke. Scoop out the choke with a knife and cut the remaining part of the artichoke into bite sizes. Dip each piece into the sauce and enjoy it.

After having selected wine at a restaurant, the waiter usually pours a small amount into the host's glass and awaits its approval. This sip is not to determine if the host likes his selection, but to find out whether or not the wine has turned to vinegar. Reject it only if it has spoiled.

Q. When proceeding by a receiving line, who goes first?
A. In the Army, Navy, Marine Corps, and Coast Guard the spouse goes first, in the Air Force, the officer.

Q. Should I shake hands with everyone in the receiving line?
A. Everyone except the aide or adjutant.

Q. If my name is mispronounced, is it rude to correct it?
A. No, by all means do so.

Q. What is the difference between a receiving line and reception line?
A. A receiving line is made up of the host, hostess, and the honorees who receive. The reception line consists of the guests being received.

Q. When planning a reception, how many should I ask to be in the receiving line?
A. There should be, in addition to the adjutant or aide, the host, hostess, and guests of honor. It should be as short as possible.

RECEPTIONS AND RECEIVING LINES

Receptions are commonplace in the services and need not be thought of as a bore, but can be anticipated with pleasure if you are self-assured and know what to do. Normally there will be a receiving line in order to create a systematic manner by which all of the guests will be assured an orderly opportunity to greet the honored guests, host, and hostess.

Usually, the invitation states which uniform the officer shall wear.

The ladies' dress is determined by the time of day. In the afternoon, a suit, pants suit or simple dress will be considered appropriate. After retreat and early evening, wear cocktail type clothing. The later the reception, the more formal the dress.

RECEPTION LINE

The guests should arrive a few minutes before the prescribed hour in order to check wraps, put out cigarettes, etc. They should then form a column of twos — officers standing on the side nearest the receiving line. An exception is an Air Force reception line, in which case the spouse stands on the side nearest the receiving line. Guests line up in order of arrival; however, it is polite to invite a very senior guest, who has arrived later than you, to precede you in the line. Never smoke in a reception line, and don't join the party until after you have been received by the host and hostess.

The officers step up to the aide or adjutant and introduce first, the spouse, and then themselves, stating their names regardless of how well they may know the aide. "Mrs. Edwards, Major Edwards." The spouse always precedes the officer except at an Air Force reception and at the White House. It is more gracious to slide by sideways instead of turning your back to your spouse.

As you pass by the receiving line, exchange brief greetings; but never engage in lengthy conversations. "How do you do?" will be sufficient. Save the chatting for later when the receiving line has disbanded.

Continue to the far side of the room; greet your friends and enjoy yourself.

Normally, the receiving line should be formed from right to left, although sometimes this may not be practical. From "right to left" means that an officer stands to the right of the spouse and the spouse to the left of the officer. This permits the American flag to be first in the flag line as well as on its own right.

The order of the receiving line could be: the aide, host, hostess, guest of honor, spouse, and then the other honorees, according to rank.

Sometimes it might be: aide, senior officer, visiting dignitary, the dignitary's spouse, the senior officer's spouse.

If civilians are asked to be in the receiving line, the host indicates their positions. A retired officer follows an officer of the same rank who is on active duty, but precedes an officer of less rank.

It may be advisable to invite an extra man to stand last in the receiving line to avoid having a woman at the end of the line.

Standing in a receiving line for a long time can be very fatiguing, and thought should be given to details that will ease the physical strain.

Be sure that a carpet is placed where those in the receiving line can stand on it.

Some say that wearing support hose helps prevent leg fatigue. Be sure that your shoes are comfortable and that your stockings don't bind your toes.

Remove rings from your right hand in order to protect your fingers.

Some women, when standing in a receiving line at the club, prefer to wear gloves as they prevent a buildup of moisture when shaking so many hands. Too, there is generally little opportunity to wash their hands after the line has disbanded. Gloves keep the hands clean, ready to enjoy refreshments. In one's own home, the hostess is usually bare-handed as washing her hands presents no problem. In either case, one does what one wants to do. When gloves are worn, they should be removed to eat, drink, or smoke.

Remember to smile.

When the aide is given a guest's name, he introduces the guest to the host. The host shakes hands and greets the guest, then introduces the person next to him, and so on down the line. As a guest is introduced, take time to listen to the name, and repeat it with a quick comment or two. However, take special care not to slow the movement of the reception line. When greeting a guest, be careful not to pull the guest down the line with your handshake.

At an exceptionally large reception, plan on those in the receiving line resting every 15 or 20 minutes.

Place the National flag and the distinguishing flags in a line centered behind the receiving line. Put the National flag at the right of the flag line, meaning at the right of the receiving line as it faces the reception line — on its own marching right. If there are senior representatives of foreign nations in the receiving line, the foreign national flags are placed immediately to the left of the U.S. National flag in English alphabetical order of the nations. The distinguishing flags are next to the foreign flags, their places being determined by seniority of the units' organizational dates. The "star" flags of generals and admirals are placed next, at the left end of the line, in their respective order of rank. Never use more than one flag per grade, regardless of how many officers of that particular grade are in the line.

WAYS TO FORM RECEIVING LINES:

(1)

FLAG LINE

A	B	C	D

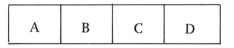

3	4	5	6	7
		CARPET		

(2)

FLAG LINE

A	B	C	D

3	4	6	7	5
		CARPET		

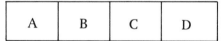

       A. U.S. National Flag
       B. Foreign National Flags
           (English alphabetically) ·
       C. Organizational Flags
       D. Generals' or Admirals' Flags

			AIR FORCE
1.	Guest (officer)	1.	Guest (spouse)
2.	Guest (spouse)	2.	Guest (officer)
3.	Adjutant or Aide	3.	Aide
4.	Host	4.	Visiting Dignitary
5.	Hostess	5.	Spouse
6.	Honored guest (officer)	6.	Host
7.	Honored guest (spouse)	7.	Hostess

CARDS

Q. If we should make a call at the home of the commanding officer, how many cards do we leave?

A. When calling on Colonel and Mrs. Whitney, the officer would leave two cards; a female spouse, one and a male spouse, two.

Q. When should we leave our cards, as we arrive or when we depart?

A. Whenever it is inconspicuous and convenient.

Q. If a card tray can't be found, what do we do with our cards?

A. Leave them on a table.

Q. What should I do if I don't have cards to leave?

A. Make your call and say nothing about it.

Q. What should we talk about when calling on a new commanding officer and his wife?

A. Keep your subjects strictly social. Save the complaints. Remember the commanding officer has been in the service for many years, and will be able to lead the conversation.

Q. Are there certain other calls that I should make?

A. You should call on a new neighbor, a new mother, a sick friend, a friend who has had a death in the immediate family, and those who have called on you.

Q. When should I call on new neighbors?

A. It is nice to call on them as soon as possible, as there might be something you can do to help them get settled. It need not be an afternoon call but stop by at any time that you think convenient.

Q. Should I leave a card when calling on a new neighbor?

A. It is helpful to the new neighbor if you do. Seeing your name written will help the neighbor remember you.

Q. As a newcomer am I expected to return the call of a neighbor who has "dropped in"?

A. Yes. This is a wonderful way to show your appreciation and a good way to make new friends.

Q. Should we pay a call on the commanding officer before leaving on a permanent change of station?

A. It is done more frequently in some branches of the services than others. The officer should inquire as to the commander's policy. If it is the custom, stay only 15 or 20 minutes; leave your cards and depart. (Put p.p.c. in the lower left-hand corner. This stands for *"pour prendre congé,"* which translates — to take leave.)

CARDS

Calling cards are not used as frequently as they were in the past. Possibly this is because many restricted their use to formal calls, and fewer formal calls are being made. Actually, an officer's card could be to the officer what a businessman's card is to the businessman. Both identify them, show who they represent, and give their status.

Cards can also be used to accompany gifts, to issue and answer invitations and for short messages. But, best of all, they can be given to a new acquaintance so he will see your name written and remember you.

Calling cards may be engraved, printed, or hand written. Engraving is considered in better taste. Officers' cards should be about 3 1/8 inches long and 1 5/8 inches wide; the actual size varies among the services. The paper should be white and the ink black. A script typeface is preferable to block letters. The full name should be used. Initials are used only when there is a special reason.

When arriving at a new assignment, the officer should inquire about the policy of making a social call at the commander's home.

If you are a commander who prefers calls made at home, remember the details that will make the calls easier for your juniors.

Turn on the porch light so that the guest will feel expected and welcomed, and place a card tray in a conspicuous place. It is the responsibility of the host and hostess to lead the conversation. Select subjects that will assist you in knowing and remembering your guests — children, parents, school, previous posts, the trip to this new assignment.

When being called on by company grade officers, if occupying government quarters, some commanders offer a tour of their home. This may be one of the few times that a younger couple has the opportunity to see field grade quarters until they are a field grade family.

You may or may not serve a beverage. Do as you wish.

After 30 minutes or so when the guests mention that they should leave, the host should not encourage them to stay longer. "It's been so nice talking to you, Mrs. Bowman. I know you'll love Fort Blank. Good night." They will leave.

The names of your guests, with reminding notes written in a note book, will help you remember them. If visiting cards were left, notes could be written on one of the cards.

In some branches of the services, the commanding officer holds a New Year's Day Reception. Attendance is mandatory. This is considered as the yearly "all calls made and returned."

```
┌─────────────────────────────────────────┐
│                                         │
│                                         │
│          James Henry Alt                │
│                                         │
│                  Lieutenant             │
│               United States Army        │
│                                         │
└─────────────────────────────────────────┘
```

Titles (rank) of junior officers are placed in the lower right hand corner, centered above the service designation.

Senior officers have a choice. They may use the above positioning or, they may prefer to have their title precede their name.

A female spouse uses her husband's full name. Traditionally, her cards are slightly larger than his.

```
┌─────────────────────────────────────────┐
│                                         │
│                                         │
│                                         │
│          Major Craig Edwards            │
│                                         │
│             United States Air Force     │
│                                         │
└─────────────────────────────────────────┘
```

It is customary in the services to introduce one's self if there is the slightest possibility of not being remembered. State your name and remind the individual where you met before; "Mrs. Whitney, I am Jim Alt. My wife, Ann, and I were stationed with you and Colonel Whitney in Germany."

People are sometimes influenced subconsciously by your choice of words. The use of certain words or phrases indicate one's degree of sophistication or lack of it. Be selective in your vocabulary. Enunciate well. Develop an attractive voice, and laugh. Listen to yourself on a tape recorder and find out if you like what you hear.

Slang and vulgarity are always best left unsaid.

Don't use initials and abbreviations to newcomers. They probably have no idea of the meaning of BOQ, AYA, NCO-WC, VIP, PWOC, CWOC, AWAF, OWC, etc., etc.

Dependents should never discuss the officer's job and should not relay tales of business personalities to their friends. If an officer is fortunate enough to have a family with whom he can air his problems, the family should take special care not to betray his trust by discussing his affairs with others.

In like manner, military dependents should never insist that their friends talk about their sponsor's affairs.

A dependent should never make fun of or criticize the spouse in public. The spouse should never be quoted on business matters.

Personal family affairs should remain personal.

A wife should never speak of "My Girls." No one likes to feel owned. Say instead, "The ladies of the medical section," or "The women in our group".

It is certainly not in good taste to hear dependents talk about "date of rank".

Never, under any circumstances, publicly criticize the commander's wife. If you don't agree with her, discuss it with her privately.

When MAKING a social telephone call say, "This is Helen Whitney calling." You should receive an answer of "Hello, Mrs. Whitney"- not "Hello, Helen" unless you are on first name basis with her. Try not to make calls during mealtime or after 9 P.M.

When you make a telephone call to a person who is not at home and a child or employee answers the phone, say, "Please tell Mrs. Bowman that Mrs. Whitney called," not that, "Helen" called.

Restrict your telephone calls to five minutes. Make appointments over the phone, and do your real chatting in person. Having long conversations on the telephone is a bad and hard-to-break habit.

If you have dialed a wrong number restrain your frustration and politely ask the recipient to excuse you. Remember, you called and disturbed him and he doesn't deserve your ire.

One should always be prompt in answering invitations with R.s.v.p. The majority of invitations are informal and require only a casual note. Informals are excellent for this as are visiting cards. You may also telephone your reply. However, numerous phone calls can inconvenience your hostess who is busy preparing for her guests but she does need to know as soon as possible how many to expect. The importance of answering, one way or another, can not be over stressed. They MUST be answered.

It might be wise for dependents to remember that they are not members of the club. The officer is the member and the dependents are the officer's guests.

If you accompany your spouse to a unit party for enlisted persons you should arrive a little late and stay only a short while.

A guest book, placed by your front door, can become one of your most cherished mementos. Signatures of today's friends and acquaintances may someday be autographs of renowned personalities. If arranged alphabetically with dates, it will be easier and more enjoyable in later years.

When invited to a wedding or a party, do not take children or friends unless they were explicitly invited. An invitation addressed to Major and Mrs. Edwards means just that and does not include the rest of the family.

When attending a church wedding, the female guest should wait for the usher to approach her and offer his arm. He will accompany her to her seat, as her escort follows behind them, down the aisle to the pew where they are to sit.

When an officer or spouse is out of town, the neighbors should make a particular effort to see to the well-being of the one remaining at home.

At all times the spouse should know where the important family papers and records are kept.

A wife should be as self-sufficient as possible. She should not depend upon her husband to take time from his duties to escort her to the commissary, dispensary, exchange, etc. She should learn to drive or use the local bus service. Many wives organize car pools for their weekly shopping. This training prepares them to be self reliant during the times when a husband must be separated from his family.

Seldom do you hear the wife of a general or admiral complain. Possibly this could be a contributing factor to her husband's success.

Civilian guests should be briefed on military customs before attending a military function.

A thoughtful person will not sit at or lean on someone else's desk, either in an office, or in a home. If you need to use the phone or some item on the desk, stand at the side of the desk to use it.

Knock before entering a closed door.

Make it a point not to handle bric-a-brac or objects of art in a friend's home. Look but don't touch. And of course it is indeed very rude to turn a plate or silver upside down to determine its quality.

It is in poor taste to ask your friends what they paid for something.

Don't ask to borrow someone's comb, brush, lipstick, or other personal belongings.

For obvious reasons, you shouldn't comb your hair in either the kitchen or the dining room. Actually, it should be done in the bedroom or the bathroom.

Gum chewing is not done at reviews, churches, cocktail parties, or other social gatherings.

Avoid serving greasy or dripping foods at any indoor party. Save them for outdoor or patio entertaining.

Under some conditions a spouse may be allowed certain privileges because of the officer's position. Basically, these privileges are permitted in order to assist the officer in conducting official duties. The spouse, at times, will be allowed to share some of them. Accept them gratefully and remember that they are privileges granted to you only because you are the spouse of the officer.

Because of her husband's vast and varied involvements, the commanding officer's wife has many responsibilities, some that are obvious to you, others unknown to you; some that are pleasant and fun, others that are trying and occasionally tragic. Give her the understanding and loyalty that she needs and realize that she, like you, is only doing her best to give and get the most out of life.

When an officer has a position as a staff officer, his wife has a definite responsibility towards the command. She should offer to help the commander's wife with official social functions even though she and her husband may not be invited. She should be prepared to accept last minute invitations (without hurt feelings) at times when the hostess needs someone to "fill in," etc. The staff wives are the women upon whom the commander's wife relies and who are considered part of the "official team."

The executive or deputy officer's wife will no doubt be closer than other women to the commander's wife. It will be her job to assist and relieve the commander's wife of as much responsibility as possible. Knowing that the commander's wife will be subject to frequent criticism, the executive officer's wife should do her best to put her in acceptable, agreeable situations and help create an amiable image in the eyes of others. The senior wife should not be "put on the spot." Neither should she find it necessary to display authority.

Because military people are often transferred, they are apt to have, or to be, house guests frequently. If you plan to see friends enroute to your next assignment, let the host and hostess know when they can expect you. Equally important, let them know when you plan to leave. It is embarrassing if they must ask you.

Try to arrive after lunch, preferably in the late afternoon.

If you are traveling with animals, ask your host in advance to make reservations for your pets at the local animal motel. This leaves him free to invite your animals if that is his preference.

If you imbibe in spirits, arrive with a bottle of your favorite and add it to their bar.

Pick up after yourself and empty your ash trays if you smoke. When you use something around the house, put it back where you found it. If you break something take it in your stride but try to replace it. Be sure to let your host or hostess know that it was broken.

Before making a long distance phone call, ask the operator to phone back the charges and leave that amount by the phone, not a "guess-timation."

Offer to help in the kitchen.

Eat what has been prepared for you. Make an attempt at everything unless you have allergies or special requirements. If you do, bring you own "care" package and provide for your particular needs.

When you need to do laundry, take it to a laundromat without discussing it with your host or hostess. With you as their guest, their demand on the machine has doubled.

As a guest, suggest going to bed at a reasonable hour. Your host and hostess have their daily routines the next day.

At night, remove the bed spread from the bed, fold it and place it on a chair.

When you are ready to leave, place your soiled sheets and towels unfolded, on a chair in the bedroom and put the bed spread back on the bed.

If there is a maid, put her name and "Thank you" on one of your cards and leave it with a few dollars on the dresser.

Most house guests, after they have left, send a small gift to their host and hostess with a "thank you" note.

The wise host and hostess will not relinquish their own bedroom to the guests. The confusion this creates makes both couples uncomfortable and can lead to strained relations.

Q. What should a woman wear to a morning coffee?

A. A simple dress, suit, slacks or sweater and skirt.

Q. From whom should I seek advice as to what I should wear to a party?

A. Your dress should be determined by the time of day and the desire of the hostess as indicated on the invitation. If you are still in doubt, ask your hostess. At an official function when the wife of the commanding officer will act as hostess, ask the executive officer's wife.

Q. Is a ball formal or informal?

A. A ball is the most formal of all dances and usually begins late in the evening.

Q. What is semiformal for a lady?

A. There is no such dress. Your dress is casual, informal, or formal.

Q. Should a military guest at a wedding wear a uniform or civilian clothes when the groom is in uniform?

A. Either is correct. However, the bride and groom have shown their preferences by having a military wedding and probably would prefer their guest to be in uniform.

Q. What is meant by "Black Tie"?

A. The hostess is asking the gentlemen to wear dinner jackets, (tuxedos) or a corresponding uniform. A dinner jacket should not be worn before 1800 hours.

Q. Is it necessary for me to wear black at a funeral?

A. No, but you should dress inconspicuously.

Frequently, when a woman receives an invitation to a social function one of her first thoughts is "How do I dress?"

Fashions and styles change but one's dress is determined by many factors, among which are: local customs; what is becoming to the individual; what one can afford; the type of invitation received; and the time of day.

For the morning — coffees, committee meetings, etc. — slacks, sweater and skirt, or a simple dress will be in good taste.

For luncheons, suits (slacks or skirts) or dresses may be worn.

For a tea or reception (3 to 5:30) your costume could be dressier with more elaborate accessories.

Cocktail or early evening affairs will call for cocktail clothes as suggested by the fashion world. This usually means more spectacular materials and designs.

For a formal dance or ball, an evening gown is in order. This is the time for you to wear your most glamourous creation.

If you receive an invitation which is either engraved or hand-written *in the third person,* for an affair that starts after six, you know it is a formal invitation. Generally speaking, the later the party begins, the more formal the dress should be.

If you receive an invitation for dinner after six, which *is not written in the third person* and the dress was not specified, wear casual cocktail clothing or a very simple long dress.

Invitations usually have one of three phrases on them: Casual, Informal, or Black Tie. These indicate how the men should dress. A woman's dress should conform to that of her escort.

Casual	sports shirt with collar, no tie

Informal	daytime
	    sports jacket or business suit with tie
	after 6 p.m.
	    business suit with tie

Black Tie (formal)	tuxedo

Some communities accept business suits instead of tuxedos.

On rare occasions, an invitation may state, "White Tie." This indicates a very elaborate evening affair and full dress (usually called a "set of tails") is requested. This outfit is entirely different from the tuxedo and most men rent them for those infrequent occasions. Female spouses would then wear evening dresses with gloves that reach well above the elbows (called eighteen button gloves).

The correct uniform is proper at all times.

If your invitation is to a costume party, or indicates sport shirts will be in order, be sure some effort is made to cooperate with your hostess' plans. If an officer arrives in coat and tie, when asked to wear a sport shirt, the hostess may feel it is his way of expressing disapproval of informality.

When you are invited to a party, regardless of what time of day it begins, make a special effort to be at your best. Your hostess has spent time preparing for you and will appreciate knowing that you have given thought to her party.

Be sure not to confuse casual with unkempt.

Take your cue from the fashion world, but if you find yourself dressed differently from the other guests, try not to be disturbed. Embarrassment makes one ill at ease and unattractive. It has happened many times before and to many people. Who knows, you may be setting a new style! Conversely, don't criticize someone else who has dressed differently.

Use a small pocketbook at parties. Large bags can create a problem for the hostess. At a dinner party, your bag should be placed on your lap, not on the table.

Hair curlers belong in the beauty parlor or your own bedroom, not in public.

Sunbathing should be done in your own secluded yard.

Make a special effort not to overdress — meaning too much jewelry — too much make-up — too much color — too fashionable hair style or dress, etc. It is in far better taste to be underdressed than overdressed.

Simplicity and good taste go hand in hand.

As most service people have little or no family living nearby, their military family substitutes for their real one. In many instances, the military family becomes closer than their blood kin. The Officers' Wives' Club is the pivot for these friendships. It sponsors community, charitable, welfare, and social functions. It creates opportunities for a wife to give of herself and her time for the good of others. It helps stimulate intellectual and social interests that prevent her from becoming self-centered, boring, and tiring. It assists her in developing into a woman who grows and matures, not only as her husband does, but as her contemporaries do.

To benefit fully, you should seek the membership committee chairwoman, and let it be known that you would like to join. Even though you feel that you may not benefit directly, you will indirectly. These are the women who help provide many personal services for the families of the men who work for your husband. Anything that contributes to their well being and the community also lends to the effectiveness of an officer's efforts.

Nevertheless, whether or not you do join, is entirely up to you.

However, until you have become a member and found out for yourself what that particular club has to offer you, and know all possible options, you can not make an unprejudiced or meaningful decision. Until then, you have made no decision at all.

Some clubs are better than others, and some have more to offer one person than another person. Join. Then if you don't like what you see, resign. You will be happier, knowing that you have exercised your freedom of choice based on your then-unbiased knowledge.

If it is your decision not to be a member, don't criticize the club to others. Obviously it does have a meaning to the many women who enjoy and need what the club has to offer.

Most clubs have monthly luncheons. These are primarily social gatherings, frequently offering entertainment of some sort. In addition to the monthly luncheon, many conduct weekly bridge sessions, golf groups, painting classes and other specialized interests, depending upon the desires of the members.

The committee chairwomen of these groups, along with the elected and honorary officers, normally comprise the executive board. It is at the executive board meetings that most of the club business is conducted.

The most successful women's clubs are usually those that conduct their executive board meetings in an informal manner. This seems to be more conducive to the members developing friendships and enjoying themselves. If a meeting is too formal, it lends to an air of uncertainty and breeds ill will.

Nevertheless, it is necessary to apply a certain amount of parliamentary procedure in order to ensure control and accomplishment of business. ROBERT'S RULES OF ORDER, found in any library, is the accepted work on this subject. If you have been elected to an office, or serve on the executive board, it is advisable that you familiarize yourself with this book.

The president should call the meeting to order, after a quorum is present, and direct the secretary to read the minutes of the last meeting. After these are approved, or amended, she should call for reports from the treasurer, and the various committee chairwomen. As each report is given, the subject may be opened for discussion by any member who, after being recognized by the president, should rise and state her point of view.

After a member has made a motion in her own words, and another has seconded, the subject is open for discussion. Then a vote, or show of hands, should be taken unless it is obvious that all are in favor or the motion

Unfinished business is next discussed, followed by new business. Any motion should be seconded and acted upon by either acclamation or vote. Following new business, the president may call for a motion to adjourn, which is then seconded and voted on by a show of hands.

Order of Business should be as follows:
1. Meeting called to order.
2. Minutes of the preceding meeting read and approved.
3. Treasurer's report.
4. Reports of committees.
5. Unfinished business.
6. New business.
7. Adjournment.

The president should not enter into debate unless she temporarily relinquishes the floor to the vice president.

Women seem inclined to change club constitutions. If at all possible, this should be avoided. Actually, a simple and easy to understand constitution will satisfy many varying needs for years to come.

A good constitution should be brief and to the point.
It should include:
> Name of the club
> Purpose of the club
> Membership requirements
> What constitutes a quorum
> Dues
> List officers and their duties
> How and when to elect officers and when they will assume their responsibility.
> How to amend the constitution
> How to disband the club, including arrangements for the dissolution of funds.

Every club should have by-laws, the rules by which the club is actually run. These should state when meetings are to be held, what committees are to be appointed, responsibilities of each, how to amend the by-laws and any other rules or regulations that are needed in running the club. Be sure that the method of amending the by-laws is easier than that of amending the constitution. Since the by-laws are the working laws, they will no doubt need to be changed more frequently.

As each member joins, she should be given a copy of the constitution and by-laws.

A yearbook, a booklet or record of the plans for the coming year, will keep your members informed. It can include the list of club activities, names of club members, dates of meetings, programs and entertainment and any other plans that will stimulate interest and increase attendance.

An honorary president is not expected to pay dues but she should not vote on an issue. However, she does pay for her luncheons. The wives' club pays for the luncheons of speakers or any other invited guests of honor.

It is customary for the vice president, with the cooperation of the executive board, to select a nominal gift of appreciation for the outgoing president. Make the presentation during the last meeting at which the president presides.

When chairing a committee, don't "go it alone" and expect others to be interested. If many are asked to assist and to be involved, the success and enthusiasm are apt to be greater.

It is an unwritten law that those attending executive board meetings do not discuss with others the happenings at the meetings.

If you have been asked to run for an office, consider it a great compliment. These are responsible respected positions within the community, and those selected are capable women. Many interesting and advantageous experiences will come your way because of it.

If you truly and sincerely must decline a nomination, it is in extremely poor taste to let it be known that you were asked. Someone else will be selected, and they certainly will not want to feel that they were second choice.

Do not allow the club's bank balance to become too large. This only helps the banker. Plan a budget; then use it.

Don't be guilty of categorizing members of the wives' club — on post, off post, regulars, reserve, retired, active, junior, senior, etc. You will only be aiding the formation of cliques and divisions. Remember that all are members of the same club and should be encouraged to be part of the same military family.

Sometimes at a club function, the junior wives will congregate among themselves while senior wives gather with other senior wives. Frequently this is misinterpreted as one group forming a clique against the other. In reality it is a normal, natural, human reaction of people to people. Junior wives have more in common with others their age and senior wives, with older women.

Every one should make an effort to mix and mingle. The responsibility belongs to no particular age group but should be shared by both the junior and senior wives. If you see a group chatting and you would like to become a part of the conversation, approach them, introduce yourself, if need be, and ask if you might join them. "Hello. I am Mary Jones. Do you mind if I join you?"

Some people are more shy than others and may need to be helped by a friend. If this is the case, you be the friend.

The wives of retired officers who join the Officers' Wives' Club have a special moral obligation to the local command. It is their responsibility to remember that the club is for the good of the community, meaning primarily, the active duty personnel. These senior members should take the viewpoint of the active duty personnel and try to understand any differences of opinion.

If the group hostessing a luncheon has decided not to reserve seats for the members, abide by its decision just as you would expect your guest to do when you are the hostess in your own home. Placing your bag on the table or tilting the chair forward in order to reserve a seat for yourself, not only ruins the efforts of those who decorated the table but also, it is indeed rude and indentifies you as being uncooperative.

Many times the wives' club will sponsor a fund raising venture for charity. It may sell merchandise or have a dinner, the cost of which may exceed its worth. Remember that this is your way of contributing to charity, and do not expect a dollar for dollar value.

Most clubs stress community and charitable support by raising money for various projects such as scouts, scholarships, etc., and this is great. However, a good leader will not lose sight of the well being of the members. They too should reap some of the benefits of their efforts. Your club should own and allow your members to enjoy attractive linen, silver and other worthwhile things that make a luncheon or meeting a real treat and a pleasure to attend. Make yours a club that women will want to join, and forget the phrase, "Do I have to join?"

An occasional free outing or luncheon for members only, may be helpful.

An annual evening affair, inviting the husbands is fun.

When a member is transferred before her term of membership expires, her valid club card is sometimes accepted as being her paid up membership in a new club.

It is advisable for the club to have its own stationery and informals.

A post office box is well worth the small yearly fee. You will avoid much lost mail and confusion by having your own box.

At club luncheons, always use a modesty skirt on the front side of the head table.

If a speech or entertainment is to follow a luncheon, let the members know fifteen minutes before it starts in order that they may do the things that make a quiet audience.

Frequently wives will have a party of some sort to bid adieu to the wife of a departing commanding officer and to welcome the wife of his replacement. These should be two separate affairs and the timing should be such that neither wife attends the party given for the other.

Suggested Head Tables at Women's Club Luncheons:

#6	#4	#2	#1	#3	#5	#7

```
┌─────────────────────────────────────────────┐
│                HEAD TABLE                     │
│                                               │
└─────────────────────────────────────────────┘
```

1. President
2. Guest of Honor or Speaker
3. Honorary President
4. Vice President
5. 2nd Vice President
6. Secretary
7. Treasurer

1. President
2. Honorary President
3. Chairwoman of Luncheon Hostess Committee

4. Vice President
5. 2nd Vice President
6. Secretary
7. Treasurer

} Some, or all, of these may relinquish their places for the other members of the Luncheon Committee.

The Treasurer may give her place to the Program Chairwoman if there is to be a program.

With Two Honored Guests:

1. President
2. Senior Honored Guest
3. Junior Honored Guest
4. Honorary President
5. Chairwoman of Luncheon Hostess Committee
6. Vice President
7. Program Chairwoman
(when there is a program)

67

COFFEE, BRUNCH, AND TEA

Q. I don't have a silver service. How can I serve coffee?

A. An attractive pottery, china or glass container is fine.

Q. At a coffee, should I serve tea in addition to coffee?

A. It is nice but not necessary. However, it is advisable to have boiling water in the kitchen for the guest who cannot drink coffee. Decaffeinated coffee has become popular and probably some of your guests would prefer it.

Q. Sometimes at a coffee there aren't enough chairs to go around. As a guest, may I get one from another room?

A. Never move furniture in someone else's home. Usually, great thought has been given to its placement and your host and hostess probably want it just as they have it.

Q. May I take my baby with me to an informal morning coffee?

A. No. Never take a child, even a baby, to an adult social function unless the hostess has specifically suggested that it be brought.

Q. What is a brunch?

A. It can be thought of as a combination of a late breakfast and an early lunch. It is usually held near midday.

Q. Should I plan on the guests sitting at the dining room table?

A. Do as you like. It may be served "sit down" or "buffet," but keep it as informal as possible.

Q. Is it acceptable to have a brunch for women only?

A. Yes. This is a wonderful idea, but be sure that it is on a day when the husbands are working.

Q. What is the difference between a tea and a reception?

A. A tea is held in the late afternoon. A reception may be held either in the afternoon or evening. A tea, whether it is a large formal party or a small informal gathering, always has a friendly, more relaxing atmosphere. A reception, which takes on a more serious air, is usually given to honor a person or an event. Frequently it is a state or military affair. There is always a receiving line at a reception.

Q. Often people joke about how to hold a teacup. Is there a certain way?

A. It is probably easier to say how not to hold it. Don't wrap your hands around the cup but place the handle between the thumb and index finger. Never put a finger through the handle. Be sure that your little finger is not crooked and always keep the saucer under the cup.

Q. Where should I put my cup and saucer when I am finished?

A. On a side table or buffet, never on the tea table.

Q. I have heard that Europeans do not pour at their teas? Is this true?

A. At most European teas an employee pours and serves the tea. Be sure when you ask some one from another country "to pour" that you explain that this is an American custom indicating friendship.

Q. If I am asked to pour, what else is expected of me? Should I arrive early to assist the hostess?

A. To be asked to pour means just that, and you need not arrive early.

Q. I have heard that in the military, coffee outranks tea. Why should one beverage outrank the other?

A. This custom grew from another - that of most American women preferring coffee to tea. Because of this, the lady serving coffee would be at the more active or popular table - a situation preferred for the honored guest. The punch table may actually be the most popular, but as it is relatively a newcomer to women's tea parties, it fell into line behind its predecessors.

COFFEE, BRUNCH, AND TEA

A coffee is a warm, informal, inexpensive, and easy way to entertain your friends. It should be simple and convey a feeling of ease.

The refreshments should not be elaborate, and much of the food may be purchased at a bakery - small donuts, coffee cake, brownies etc. Home made cinnamon toast and small hot biscuits split open with slivers of baked ham are easy to prepare.

At a small coffee held at home, ask each guest, as she arrives, to serve herself. She will sip her coffee as she mingles with the other guests. If you have asked someone "to pour," it is best to wait and serve after most of the guests have arrived so that the pourer will not have to remain at the table too long. Usually the honored or senior guest is asked. This, however, tends to add an air of formality, and a coffee is best when informal.

If you are planning a large coffee for your section or wives' club which is to be held at the club, it would be better to have a group of ladies pour. Your party will run smoothly if one person is in charge of the pouring detail.

A brunch may be thought of as a combination of breakfast and lunch - the menu leaning towards breakfast and the hour towards lunch. It should be a casual, informal, relaxing affair frequently given on the spur of the moment.

It may also be planned in advance with informal invitations telephoned or written.

For an impromptu affair, women would dress casually. But if it is a planned affair, such as "after Church on Sunday," they would dress more formally. In either case, unless the invitation states otherwise, men may wear sports jackets with slacks and save their uniforms and suits for other occasions.

Bloody Marys, white wine or cocktails are usually served, but seldom high balls. Fruit juices should be available. Egg dishes with ham or sausage, waffles, biscuits, or any "specialty of the house" may be served sit-down or buffet, but remember to be informal.

Teas should be planned in advance with details given great thought. These are occasions when you may use your best linen, silver, and china.

A white cloth is best, although a colored one is attractive when used for holidays or special occasions.

Place the tea service, with a straight chair for the pourer, at one end of the table. Both tea and coffee may be served on the same tray if the tray is large enough and the party small enough. The centerpiece and the food should be attractively arranged on the rest of the table. For a large tea, two trays are advisable, one for the coffee and the other for the tea, placing the coffee tray at the end of the table nearest the entrance and the tea at the opposite end.

The tray should not have a cloth; the service should be placed directly on the tray. There should be a pot of tea, one of boiling water to dilute the tea, milk, sliced lemon with a small fork or toothpick, lump sugar and sugar tongs. The cups should be placed on their saucers with the teaspoon to the right of the handle - easy and convenient for the lady pouring to reach. This is usually at the left of the tray.

The coffee service is much the same, but should consist of a coffee pot, lump sugar, sugar tongs, and a pitcher of cream.

Tall formal candles may be used, lighted, with curtain drawn, even though it is still daylight. This is especially delightful during the winter months or on a rainy day. Conversely, if your tea table is under the trees in your garden during the summer, candles would be out of place.

The food should be different from that used at cocktail parties. Small tea sandwiches, with crust removed, may consist of water cress, cucumbers, olives or any of the numerous lighter fillings. Thin slices of buttered bread with the crust left on are good. Tarts, cookies, petits fours, short breads, and cake may be served. Nuts, candies, and mints are good. The sandwiches are "finger foods"; but if you have a cake or a sweet that requires a fork, stack the plates near the cake with a napkin between each plate.

For a club affair, you will need to invite several ladies to pour. To be asked to pour at a tea is a great compliment, and one should thank the hostess for the honor.

Compile a list of the names of those who will be asked. Give the wife of the ranking officer position No. 1, the wife of the next ranking officer No. 2, etc. The lady whose name appears first should be asked to pour coffee; the second lady, tea; the third, punch - if there is punch - if not, she relieves the No. 1 lady. In like manner, the other pourers are relieved by the next person on the list. This rotation continues until the hostess feels it is no longer necessary.

The ladies who are to pour will appreciate being asked a day or two in advance and being given an approximate time when you would like them to be there. A written note is best as it will eliminate any possibility of confusion.

It is advisable to ask someone to ensure that the pouring sequence is followed. The wife of a very senior officer should be relieved after five minutes or so, but the others may remain ten or fifteen minutes. This coordinator will, of course, need to consult her prearranged list; but a gracious woman will keep it out of sight and not give the appearance of "running the show". This same person could also make sure that there is always sufficient tea and coffee on the trays.

The coordinator and the replacement should approach the lady who is pouring on the side opposite from where the guests are receiving their tea. As the replacement and the present pourer exchange places, the coordinator will introduce them if they have not met.

Unless she can be positive that her pocketbook will not slide from her lap, the pourer should place her bag under the skirt of the table or under her chair, making sure that the other guests will not trip over it. She then places both feet on the floor (never crosses her knees) and sits erect. As the guests pass by for their beverage, the pourer picks up a cup, on its saucer, and fills it three-quarters full. If she is pouring tea, she will ask the guest if she prefers strong or weak tea. When the answer is weak, the tea is then diluted with hot water. Next, the guest is asked if she would like sugar and how many lumps, cream, etc.

When the pourer is not pouring, she should place both hands in her lap,(no smoking, please) and wait for the next guest. If something is needed, the committee member should be notified.

The pourer should not leave the table until she is relieved by the next pourer.

After a guest has received a beverage, she should then serve herself sandwiches, cake or whatever she would like, and move from the table to another part of the room to chat with the other ladies. It is not necessary to know the other women in order to talk to them. The fact that you are all guests is sufficient. Approach them and introduce yourself.

The guests will stand as they sip their tea, but it is suggested that a few chairs be available.

Since it is not necessary to arrive at the beginning, nor stay until the end, your guests will be coming and going. Special effort should be taken to ensure that the table remains lovely throughout the tea.

If. the guest list is exceptionally long, it may be advisable to have more than one table, placing coffee on one and tea on another.

Remember to have sufficient side tables so that the ladies will have a place to put the used cups and saucers.

It is a great help to your friends if you invite their daughters, after they have reached the age of 16 or 17. It gives them social experience in an adult atmosphere. Be sure to send separate invitatins, one to the mother and another to the daughter. Remember to forget that they are younger and treat them as you do your other guests.

Since the senior wives are asked to pour at official teas, it is a good idea to ask the junior wives to pour at the smaller unit parties. Start with the most junior wife and work upward, or any other system; but be sure you stick to some sort of plan in order to avoid hurt feelings.

CHILDREN

Q. When my baby is born, should I send announcements to our friends on base?

A. No. They will know when the baby is born. Announcements with pertinent information — name, sex, weight, etc., may be sent to out-of-town friends whom you believe are really interested.

Q. Should we allow our daughter to send graduation invitations to out-of-town friends when we know that they won't be able to attend? It may look like we are asking for a present.

A. Graduation invitations are usually thought of as announcements instead of invitations. Despite the fact that friends may be seas apart, it is quite proper to send them invitations provided you sincerely feel that they are interested in the graduate.

Q. Should I correct someone else's child when he is playing with my children at my house?

A. If you are sure that you can correct him in such a polite manner that you will not hurt his feelings, then do so, letting him know that, while a guest at your house, he must abide by the rules of your house. Otherwise politely send him home. Never under any circumstances, spank, hit or physically reprimand someone else's child.

Q. May we take our baby with us to the movies? It saves the expense of a baby sitter.

A. Usually there is no regulation prohibiting it. If the baby should cry or make noises to disturb others, take it out immediately. Consider the fact that you are unnecessarily exposing your child to a theater full of germs and the risk may not be worth it.

Q. Is it all right for my children to call our neighbor by her first name?

A. Only if the neighbor has invited them to do so and if you too, approve.

CHILDREN

Do not allow your children or your dogs to run through or play in the yards of other people unless they have been invited. You are responsible for what they do, wherever they are. Even though a base or post is government property, the persons living in the quarters are entitled to privacy and the privilege of enjoying their own grounds.

Usually speed limits on military installations are lower than civilian communities. This should not encourage you to permit your children to run or play in the street. Not only is it dangerous, but it will allow your children to develop reckless and irresponsible habits that could result in disaster when you return to a civilian community where they are not as well protected.

Sometimes, a cannon salute precedes the National Anthem when hoisting or lowering the flag at Reveille or Retreat. Children should be taught to respect the flag and told that when they hear the cannon or the music, they should stop all play, stand at attention, and salute, facing in the direction of the flagstaff.

Children should be allowed to attend reviews and public affairs alone only if they are old enough and reliable enough to behave properly when unsupervised.

Don't leave small children in the car while you fill a lengthy shopping list. Use the post nursery if a neighbor can't help.

Let your children know that a theater is not a race track. The seats are there to be used. If a child can't sit quietly in a theater, then the probability is that the show is too mature, and the child belongs at home.

They should never be allowed to throw gum wrappers, bottles, or other trash on base or post. There are receptacles placed about for this purpose which should be used. If you see another's child throw paper on the ground, do not hesitate to ask him politely to pick it up. The base is your home, and your interest in keeping it clean should be respected.

Toys should not be left in driveways, sidewalks, stairways or any place where they may be destroyed or where others may trip over them.

Don't allow children to play in empty quarters, barracks or warehouse areas. Teach them the meaning of an "off limits" sign, and make sure that they obey it.

Children should be instructed in social courtesies as early as possible. Not only does this make the child more attractive, but it also aids in overcoming shyness and self-consciousness while developing poise and self-assurance.

Children old enough to read should learn the meaning of R.s.v.p. and use it themselves.

The hamburger plus the informal manner of eating make the knife and fork strangers to many of today's children. Nevertheless, the time will come when they will be adults who are expected to know how to handle table utensils. Give them the opportunity to learn table manners now rather than waiting until they are grown, when the lack of manners not only will be embarrassing but may also hold them back from whatever accomplishments they seek.

Both boys AND girls should be taught to stand when adults enter the room. They should remain standing until the adults have either been seated or left the room. Boys, of course, should continue this habit into manhood; girls until they themselves are considered adults.

Introduce your children to strangers just as you would another adult. "Mrs. Whitney, this is our son Jimmy." Teach them the proper reply. "How do you do." In like manner, they should introduce their friends. "Mother, this is Billy Whitney."

They should say "Yes sir" and "No sir" to their fathers and other men. The grunts "Huh" and "Unh-Huh" should be omitted from their vocabularies. Sir and Ma'm (or "Yes, Mrs. Whitney" or "Yes, Mother") are certainly more pleasant to hear.

Time was when children of military families answered the phone by saying "Colonel Whitney's quarters. Billy Whitney speaking." Today however, the large number of crank calls has made this inadvisable. Instead, they could say "Hello." or "Good morning. (Good afternoon etc.) May I help you?" When making a call, they should introduce themselves. "Good morning. This is Billy Whitney speaking. May I please talk to Tommy?" Be sure that children too small to be responsible do not answer the phone. It may be very cute, but it is also very irritating to phone a friend and have a small child answer and repeatedly say "Hello, hello, hello."

Give thought to an allowance. There are many opinions as to whether or not children should work for it or if it should be used as a disciplinary measure. Whatever your opinion, you should be consistent about giving it to them and never borrow from them. You will be instilling good monetary habits for which you will be thankful in the years to come.

As a child matures, a clothing allowance gives increased independence and responsibility.

Stress to your children the importance of writing "thank you notes," particularly to aunts, uncles and grandparents from whom they are frequently separated. The following fill-in can be used by the child who finds it difficult to compose a letter.

Dear_____,

Thank you so much for the_____
                    (beautiful, interesting, wonderful, needed)
_____you sent me for_____.
    (gift)   (Xmas, my birthday)
I know I will enjoy it and think of you when I use it. Most of all,

I_____your thoughtfulness.
(appreciate, treasure, value)
                                    With all my love,

_____

Most children are taught not to interrupt when adults are speaking. If you are talking when a child obviously would like to speak, encourage it by interrupting yourself as soon as reasonable. "Excuse me, Helen, but I believe Billy has something important to say."

Never raise your voice to your children. They will be more apt to listen to a person who is soft spoken and difficult to hear than to one who screams and hollers. Rest assured that if you shout at them, they will shout at you.

Say nice things about your children, possibly when they can over-hear you. If you don't speak well of them, who will?

Many families routinely have Sunday dinner at the club. This gives the children experience in an adult world and a weekly opportunity to "dress up."

Some families set aside one day a month for a formal meal at home. Everyone dresses for dinner, candles are lit and the meal is served as you would to your guests. Among other things, your children learn that nice things can happen at home.

Frequent baby showers can become a burden. Many commanders' wives have established the precedent of only one such shower for each first born, given jointly by the other ladies of the group. Some commanders' wives select for their husbands a modest gift which they give to each new baby. It means much to young parents to have a keepsake from the commanding officer for the baby. An inexpensive baby spoon is ideal.

Politeness is the key to most successful family relationships. If parents are polite to children and children are polite to parents and brothers and sisters, a happier home life can not help but exist.

It is to your advantage and to that of your children for you to keep your family immunization records up to date. When orders are received for an overseas assignment, it is easier on everybody if their shots have not lapsed, and they need not begin a new series.

Because you are transferred more often in the service, special effort should be made to instill in your children the responsibility of contributing to the betterment of their home. Home is where their family and love are, even though their house may change frequently.

Show patience and understanding to others as they too, learn and mature. People more often need help than criticism.

Depend upon the judgment of others and accept their ways, even though they may be different from yours. One should always show respect to age and authority, and kindness and consideration to every one.

To truly gracious people, there will be many times when they feel the proper thing to do, will be the incorrect one.

Sometimes it is better to do the wrong thing graciously than the proper thing rudely.

Let this book be a yardstick as you stride along with the established customs and traditions. Use it as a reference book; but remember, none of us can always do everything perfectly. Knowing this, do not hesitate to venture forth with self-assurance and the knowledge acquired from this book. Time and experience are great teachers.